The Potter's House

Interpretation & Applications

By

E. W. Bullinger, D.D.

ISBN: 978-1-78364-552-7

www.obt.org.uk

****

THE OPEN BIBLE TRUST
Fordland Mount, Upper Basildon,
Reading, RG8 8LU, UK

The Potter's House
Interpretation & Applications

Contents

Page

Introduction

Introduction

"The word which came to Jeremiah from the LORD, saying, Arise, and go down to the potter's house, and there I will cause thee to hear my words. Then I went down to the potter's house, and behold he wrought a work on the wheels. And the vessel that he made of clay was marred in the hand of the potter: so he made it again another vessel, as it seemed good to the potter to make it" (Jer. 18:1-4).

A great Divine principle is wrapped up in these verses. The lesson to be learned in the potter's house is a lesson, not only for all time, but for eternity. It reaches back to the past, and on to the future, embracing all departments of revealed Truth.

To learn this truth and understand this lesson it is necessary to distinguish carefully between *Interpretation* and *Application*. The Interpretation is one; but the Applications are many.

The work which Jeremiah saw in the potter's house, and the words which he heard there, are alike full of precious instruction.

The Divine lesson there taught is this:

GOD NEVER MENDS WHAT MAN HAS MARRED.
HE ALWAYS SUBSTITUTES HIS OWN NEW PROVISION.

The Interpretation of this passage belongs to Israel,
As is clearly shown by the context; for it goes on to say, "Then the word of the Lord came to me, saying, O house of Israel, cannot I do with you as this potter? saith the Lord."

Israel was this first vessel in the hands of the potter. As a nation, Israel is "marred;" and in the "other" vessel we are shown that it is not God's purpose to mend the old nation thus marred; but to "scatter" it, and "pluck up," and "pull down" the kingdom: and afterwards to "build and to plant" – not the old nation, but a new nation, that should bring forth fruits worthy of God's Kingdom. This great fact is more clearly stated by our Lord in Matt. 21:43: "The kingdom of God shall be taken from you and given to a nation bringing forth the fruits thereof."

These words are conclusive; as was also the interpretation of the Scripture which said, "The stone which the builders rejected, the same is become the head of the corner: this is the Lord's doing, and it is marvellous in our eyes."

The old nation of Israel rejected Christ, the Stone. But a time is coming when He will become the Head over a new nation, who will say, "Blessed is He that cometh in the name of the Lord." He has "miserably destroyed those wicked men and will let out his vineyard unto other husbandmen which shall render to him the fruits in their seasons" (Matt. 21:41).

"The vineyard of the Lord of hosts is the house of Israel, and the men of Judah His pleasant plant" (Isa. 5:7).

Not yet, therefore, is that vineyard let out to those other husbandmen. Not yet is the kingdom given to the nation that will bring forth its fruits. The kingdom is yet in abeyance: The King is yet "henceforth expecting:" He is not yet made "the head of the corner.

The old Israel did not obtain what it sought for; but the election hath obtained it (Rom. 11:7). And the new Israel, the "other vessel," will be as the potter shall be pleased to make it. He has told us how He will make it. He hath said that when He shall have planted His pleasant plant in its own vineyard,

> "Then will I sprinkle clean water upon you,
> And ye shall be clean:
> From all your filthiness, and from all your idols,
> Will I cleanse you.
> A new heart also will I give you,
> And a new spirit will I put within you:
> And I will take away the stony heart out of your flesh,
> And I will give you a heart of flesh.
> And I will put my spirit within you
> And cause you to walk in my statutes
> And ye shall keep my judgments and do them
> And ye shall dwell in the land that I gave to your fathers;
> And ye shall be my people,
> And I will be your God" (Ezek. 36:25-28).

Here we see the nation that will possess the kingdom: and here we have the fruits which it will bring forth.

Interpreters appropriate all these blessings to themselves and rob Israel of the promises specially made to them.

One set says that, Anglo-Israel is the nation of Matt. 21:43, though we look in vain for the fruits proceeding from an indefectible nature.

Another set says that, Christians now have the blessings of Ezek. 36; and, though they fail to bring forth such fruits, they think they will be able to do so if they only follow the teachings and obey the precepts of those who preach the new "Gospel of surrender."

But not so may the Word of Truth be wrongly divided. Anglo-Israelism is not in Matt. 21:43. And the Church is not in Ezek. 36.

The lesson to be learned in the potter's house belongs to the Olive Tree of Rom. 11. The Tree is not cut down. Only some of the old branches are "broken off." But the Election, *i.e.,* the Remnant, is yet to be grafted in, "for God is able to graft them in again."

This, then, is the interpretation of the potter's house as it concerns Israel.

But there are, as we have said, several *applications* of this Divine principle; which runs through the whole of Scripture and permeates every department of truth.

The Lord never repairs what man has ruined; or mends what man has marred.

He makes Him again another vessel, as it pleaseth Him to make it.

There are no less than *eight* applications which we may study with profit.

1.
The Covenants

1. The Covenants

The first Covenant was stated in these words: "It shall be our righteousness, if we observe to do all these commandments before the Lord our God as He hath commanded us" (Deut. 6:25).

But Israel broke this covenant. It was "marred." And it is not in God's plan to mend the old covenant. No. He will make a new one. And it will be made with the New Nation of Israel. For it is written:-

> "Behold, the days come, saith the Lord,
> That I will make a new covenant,
> With the house of Israel, and with the house of Judah:
> Not according to the covenant that I made with their fathers,
> In the day that I took them by the hand
> To bring them out of the land of Egypt;
> Which My Covenant They Brake,
> Although I was an husband unto them, saith the Lord:
> But this shall be the covenant which I will make with the house of Israel;
> After those days, saith the Lord,
> I will put my law in their inward parts,
> And write it in their hearts;
> And will be their God,
> And they shall be my people.
> And they shall teach no more every man his neighbor,
> And every man his brother,
> Saying, Know the Lord:
> For they shall all know me,
> From the least of them unto the greatest of them,

Saith the Lord:
For I will forgive their iniquity,
And I will remember their sin no more" (Jer. 31:31-34).

"Which my covenant they brake." And, that being so, we have the Divine comment on this in Heb. 8:7. "If that first covenant had been faultless, then should no place have been sought for the second." The first vessel that the potter made was marred. So He will make a new vessel. "In that he saith, A new covenant, he hath made the first old. Now that which decayeth and waxeth old is ready to vanish away" (Heb. 8:13).

Nothing can make the lesson of the potter's house more clear as it touches the Covenants[1].

Both belong to Israel. The one is forever past. It waxed old and has vanished away. The other is not yet made. It will be made with that New Israel to which the *interpretation* belongs. The Church has nothing to do with that "New Covenant." We are now under an unconditional covenant of grace; of which it is written, "by the works of the law shall no flesh be justified" (Gal. 2:16). We have more than that New Covenant: for we have Christ, and possessing Him, we possess all in Him.

---

[1] For more on covenants, see Appendix 1.

2.
Ordinances

2. Ordinances

With the Old Covenant go all the ordinances that pertained to it, even those which were of Divine institution.

They were all marred by man; and will never be mended by God. The prophet describes to us how they were marred:

> "To what purpose is the multitude of your sacrifices unto me?
> Saith the Lord:
> I am full of the burnt offerings of rams, and the fat of fed beasts;
> And I delight not in the blood of bullocks, or of lambs, or of he-goats.
> When ye come to appear before me,
> Who hath required this at your hand, to trample my courts?
> Bring no more vain oblations;
> Incense is an abomination unto me,
> New moon and sabbath, the calling of assemblies-
> I cannot away with (*i.e.* tolerate) iniquity and the solemn meeting:
> Your new moons and your appointed feasts my soul hateth;
> They are a trouble unto me,
> I am weary to bear them" (Isa. 1:11-14, R.V.).

This is what Ordinances had become long before the days of the Lord Jesus. This is how that beauteous vessel was marred.

And, are they to be repaired or re-adjusted and improved? No. Hear the Divine lesson from the potter's house in Heb. 10:6-9.

"In burnt-offerings and sacrifices for sin thou has had no pleasure. Then said I

LO, I COME

(in the volume of the book it is written of me,) to do thy will, O God.

"Above when he said, Sacrifice and offering and burnt offerings and offering for sin thou wouldest not, neither hadst pleasure therein; which are offered by the law; then said he, Lo, I come to do thy will, O God. HE TAKETH AWAY THE FIRST, THAT HE MAY ESTABLISH THE SECOND."

Yes, the first is taken away; and, blessed be God, the second is *established* forever.

God has not "taken away" His own ordinances that He may establish man's. Far from it. What He will establish is the substance, which is Christ, and not the shadow (Col. 2:17). He blotted out "the handwriting (or bond) of Ordinances that was against us, which was contrary to us, and took it out of the way, nailing it to his cross" (Col. 2:14).

"We, when we were children, were in bondage under the religious ordinances[2] of the world" (Gal. 4:3). But now, we, being delivered

---

[2] This is the meaning of the word (*stoicheia*) which occurs four times in the Church Epistles: twice in Galatians (4:3, 9), and twice in Colossians (2:8, 20). In Gal. it is rendered "elements" in the text, and *rudiments* in the margin, while in Col. It is rendered "rudiments" in the text, and *elements* in the margin. The R.V. has the latter in all four places.

from doing service unto them which by nature are no gods, are asked, "Why turn ye again to the weak and beggarly religious ordinances whereunto ye desire AGAIN to be in bondage?"

And to show what sort of bondage this is, He goes on to say, "Ye observe[3] days, and months, and times, and years; I am afraid of you, lest I have bestowed on you labour in vain" (Gal. 4:8-11).

The nature of some of these is indicated in Col. 2:16, when he says, "Let no man therefore judge you in meat or in drink, or in respect of an holy day, or of the new moon, or of the Sabbath." (See also Rom. 14:5, 6).

In Col. 2:8 we are warned not to be deceived by vain philosophy, or to follow the *tradition* of men, and observe their religious ordinances; and are asked, "If ye died (*i.e.,* died once for all: not "be dead," as A.V.) with Christ from the religious observances of the world, why, as though living in the world, are ye subject to ordinances after the commandments and doctrines of men . . . which all are to perish with the using?" (Col. 2:20).

Here we have the lesson of the potter's house with regard to ordinances; and solemn and far-reaching it is. All ordinances have been marred by man, and now they have been "taken away," "abolished," and "blotted out." The "shadow" has been replaced by Christ; and, being "complete in Him," ordinances can do nothing for us except to hinder our apprehension of that completeness.

---

[3] The word translated "observe" is always used in a bad sense in the New Testament.

3.
The Priesthood

3. The Priesthood

The Priesthood also has been marred: and therefore done away. The Levitical priesthood after the order of men has failed, and it is not in God's purpose to recognize any human priests again. He is not going to make an improved order of human priests. They are all abolished, as it is written, "If therefore perfection were by the Levitical priesthood, (for under it the people received the law), what further need was there that another priest should rise after the order of Melchisedec, and not be called after the order of Aaron? . . . For He testifieth Thou art a Priest forever after the order of Melchisedec. For there is verily a disannulling of the commandment going before for the weakness and unprofitableness thereof . . . And they truly were many Priests, because they were not suffered to continue by reason of death: But this man, because he continueth ever, hath an unchangeable priesthood" (Read the whole of Heb. 7:11-28).

The priestly vessel has been marred. A new priest has been appointed, after a different order, under a better covenant, and bringing in a better hope. That Priest is Christ. He is God's new provision for man's failure.

Any attempt, therefore, now, to set up any order of human priests is a direct reversal of God's plan. It is open rebellion against Him, and against His Christ. It ignores His provision, and despises His Word, in which He has explained the whole matter to us in Heb. 7.

4.
The Kings

4. The Kings

It is the same with the kings. These also failed. They used the power delegated to them for their own interests; and, for the most part against God.

The Royal Vessel has been marred; and it is not God's purpose to improve any earthly or human order of kings. Christ absorbs all Regal rights, as He absorbs all Priestly privileges, and all earthly Ordinances.

This is the decree: "Yet have I set my king upon my holy hill of Zion." Meantime all earthly Royalty is only delegated; and, when "He shall come whose right it is," He will take all kingly power into His own hands, and wield it to the glory of God, and the welfare of man.

5.
Man

5. Man

We see the same eternal principle with regard to man. He also was marred; and, in Gen. 3, we see the marring fraught with so much evil and misery, sin and death.

We need no further Scripture for this. But we need to learn the all-important lesson of the potter's house, that man is incapable of improvement.

It is not God's purpose to mend that which is marred. The first Adam fell irretrievably; and no descendant of his can rise above the level of the old Adam, who was lost and ruined in his fall.

Another man has been substituted for him: "the second man," "the last Adam," the "new man."

It is not in God's purpose to improve the old man, but to create the new man. The old nature is irretrievably marred, beyond repair. It is "enmity against God"; it is "not subject to the law of God, neither indeed can be" (Rom. 8:7).

A new nature must be implanted, and the saved sinner baptized with the Holy Ghost into the Body of Christ. He is henceforth a new man, made "as it pleased the potter to make it": for now, God hath set the members every one of them in the Body, as it hath pleased Him" (1 Cor. 12:18).

"If any man be in Christ, he is a new creation: the old things have passed away [not been mended or improved]; behold all things are become new. And all things are of God" (2 Cor. 5:17, 18).

Henceforth, it is not the old man made better, but the new man new-created within.

6.
The Human Body

6. The Human Body

It is the same with these mortal bodies. They are the scenes of suffering, disease and death. There is no "tree of life" to keep down disease or prevent death. No eternal life, now, short of change and Rapture, or Resurrection in bodies altogether new and glorious, like Christ's own body.

True, the vessel that was "made of clay" was marred. Able to "live forever" (Gen. 3:22) it became mortal.

"It is appointed unto men once to die" (Heb. 9:27) is the solemn sentence that has been passed upon men.

"That was not first which is spiritual, but that which is natural; and afterward that which is spiritual" (1 Cor. 15:46).

"The first man is of the earth, earthy: the second man is the Lord from heaven" (1 Cor. 15:47).

Yes, "another," a new vessel must be made; and it is to be the gift of God. A house which is from heaven, a building of God, eternal in the heavens (2 Cor. 5:1, 2).

Not till we possess this glorious body can it be said "mortality is swallowed up of life." Man says it is swallowed up at death; but then, he knows nothing about it; so we need not heed him, or his traditions. We are told that "it is sown a natural body: it is raised a spiritual body" (1 Cor. 15:44). But this is not good enough for man. He cannot wait for that. He wants something between; and he not only invents it, but actually substitutes it for God's great purpose.

Man knows nothing of the lessons to be learned in the potter's house. He asks, "How?"

He asks, "How are the dead raised up? And with what body do they come?" (1 Cor. 15:35).

There is only one answer; and it is given "touching the resurrection of the dead." "Ye do err, not knowing the Scriptures, nor the power of God" (Matt. 22:29).

The great answer is that it will be "the gift of God."

God GIVETH it a body as it hath pleased Him" (1 Cor 15:38).

Nicodemus asked, with regard to that other vessel – the new creation – which is born of the Spirit: "HOW can these things be?" (John 3:9). The answer is the same: "God so loved the world that he GAVE his only begotten Son" (John 3:16).

The woman of Samaria, when the Lord commenced this new creation work within her, asked, "HOW is it that thou . . . askest drink of me?" Jesus answered, "If thou knewest the GIFT of God, and who it is that saith to thee" (John 4:9, 10).

Yes, the power of God, and the gift of God: this is the answer to all our questioning.

It settles the nature of this new vessel – "God giveth it a body as it hath pleased him." That determines all doubts; that solves all difficulties. The great Potter Himself will "return and make it another vessel as it hath pleased him." "Hath not the potter power

over the clay?" He asks. Ah! Blessed be God, that is the point –
"POWER" – the "power of God."

We patch up these poor bodies of humiliation as best we can; but
God's thoughts are higher than our thoughts. He will give a new
body "like unto Christ's glorious body" (Phil. 3:21), and this will
be forever.

"He taketh away the first, that he may establish the second." And
the "second" is always "forever."

7.
The Heavens and Earth

7. The Heavens and Earth

Here, we have a further application of this great, Divine, eternal principle. The six-days' work of creation was marred by Satan. The sentence was pronounced "Cursed be the ground": and it was cursed. "Thorns and thistles" were unknown till then; and it may be that out of that cursed ground was brought forth then, not only vegetable life, but animal, or, at least, insect life and bacteria life; the germs of disease and the causes of all suffering and sorrow. And now it is not God's purpose to mend this earth. It is man's one effort to improve it, and to bring in a Millennium without Christ: but he will never succeed. Christ did not come into the world to improve it, but to find a grave in it; that, by His precious death, His Redemption work might be fully accomplished, in virtue of which the curse will one day be removed, and a new Heaven and a new Earth will take the place of "the heavens and the earth which are now."

Another vessel is to be made; and it will be "as it pleased the potter to make it."

All God's children, who "know the scriptures," know that there is no hope for the world until He shall come and "make all things new." We know full well that there can be no Millennium without Christ.

Johosheba could not have any complacency in the political schemes, or social plans, of Athaliah. She knew that all these would come to an end, as soon as the rightful king should be manifested. Paul did not go to Thessalonica to take part in schemes of sanitation. He did not go to Ephesus to see about "the housing of the poor." He had no "Citizen Sunday"; but every Sunday and every day was for Christ. "To me to live is Christ."

It is for us now to say, "We look for new heavens and a new earth, wherein dwelleth righteousness," Righteousness can never *dwell* in this world, which is under the curse; and which has increased that guilt and curse by putting the only Righteous One to death. And yet, having done that, the world dares to talk about "righteousness" apart from Christ.

No! not until He shall come, and make all things new, will creation see righteousness dwell in the earth.

Then it will be said:

> "Mercy and truth are met together;
> Righteousness and peace have kissed each other.
> Truth shall spring out of the earth;
> And righteousness shall look down from heaven.
> Yea, the Lord shall GIVE that which is good
> And our land shall yield her increase.
> Righteousness shall go before him;
> And shall set us in the way of his steps."
>
> (Ps. 85:10-13)

"Surely his salvation is nigh them that fear him" (*v.* 9). Yes so nigh that His people now, already, enjoy by faith, by grace, and by anticipation, all these blessings *in their hearts*. For now "the kingdom of God is not eating and drinking, but righteousness, and peace and joy, in the Holy Ghost" (Rom. 14:17).

But then it will be universal and physical, and "glory will dwell in our Land."

But this brings us to our last application.

8.

The Church

8. The Church

This too has failed: Not God's purpose; but man's attempted "improvements" of it.

CORPORATE TESTIMONY HAS FAILED.

Forsaking the truth of "the one Body" in Christ (2 Tim. 1:15), men soon began to make and to be concerned about their own Bodies, and Fellowships (1 Cor. 1:3). The vessel was soon marred.

And yet man will not recognize this great and solemn fact. His one aim is corporate re-union of some kind. Roman re-union, or Plymouth re-union, or Grindelwald re-union, or Lambeth Round-Table re-union. But all are doomed to utter failure. Corporate union has gone, never to be restored. Only for a short time is the Church viewed as "the house of God": and Timothy is instructed how he is to conduct himself; and whom he is to appoint in it; and what their qualifications are to be. But in the *second* Epistle all this is gone: what was *rule* in the first Epistle becomes *ruin* in the second. Corporate position has vanished. Everything is intensely personal, and individual. All is "I" and "me," and "thou" and "thee." Paul had been forsaken, and his doctrine too. He had "fought a good fight." He is ready to be offered (2 Tim. 4:6, 7). The only successors he knew of were "grievous wolves" who would not spare the flock (Acts 20:29).

The vessel is marred beyond all repair. It is not God's purpose to "reform" it. There must be another vessel:" and thank God, we have it, in "the Christ." "He taketh away the first that he may ESTABLISH the second." Yes! That will be established forever and forever; after man's Bodies have all been dis-established. It is endowed with all the grace and gifts and glory of God; for in its Head dwelleth "all the fulness of the Godhead bodily."

This is "another vessel" indeed. Far beyond all man's powers of conception to imagine its glory and its beauty.

When once this is seen, by faith, the churches are seen to be a seething mass of conflict and confusion – the potsherds of the earth striving with the potsherds of the earth.

The churches have not learned the great lesson of the potter's house. *They* talk about the "unity of the body;" while Scripture speaks only of "the unity of the Spirit" (Eph. 4:3), which they fail so signally to manifest; and hence, they still set *corporate union* as their goal, notwithstanding all the anarchy without, and the corruption within; not discerning that it can be only corporate union *in ruin*. There is "no king in Israel." Each one does that which is right in his own eyes. Discipline is non-existent, or it is abused. Promotion is reserved for the lawless: and favour is for those who most stoutly deny the truth and inspiration of God's Word.

The churches are being destroyed by a flood: for, under the guise of "temperance," they are fast becoming submerged under a flood of worldliness; and spiritual worship is almost unknown. Under the influence of Solos and Fiddles it has become a thing of the past.

Oh! To learn lessons of the potter's house; and to be set free from man, "whose mouth speaketh vanity;" and from the "strange children," who know not the counsels of God.

Then, and only then, shall we be free to be occupied with God's purpose. We shall cease from efforts to reform or improve the vessel that has been marred; and set our hearts on the "other vessel" which is to supersede it; yea, on that "One Body" (Eph. 4:4) of which Christ is the glorious Head in Heaven, and His people with members of it on earth (1 Cor. 12).

In that Body the members are set "as it hath pleased Him." Oh! That this may be increasingly realized in our happy experience, so that it may be as it also pleaseth us.

Appendix 1
More on the
Covenants

Appendix 1
More on the Covenants

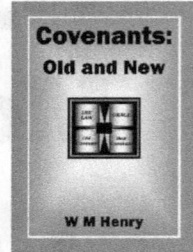

Abraham Progress in the Covenants of God
By Glen Burch

The New Covenant
By J Eustace Mills

The New Covenant
Who is it with? When is it for?
By Michael Penny

Covenants: Old and New
W M Henry

Further details of these books can be seen on www.obt.org.uk
and they can be ordered from that website.

They are also available as eBooks from Amazon and Apple and
as KDP paperbacks from Amazon.

About the Author

About the Author

Ethelbert W. Bullinger D.D. (1837-1913) was a direct descendant of Heinrich Bullinger, the great Swiss reformer who carried on Zwingli's work after the latter had been killed in war.

E. W. Bullinger was brought up a Methodist but sang in the choir of Canterbury Cathedral in Kent. He trained for and became an Anglican (Episcopalian) minister before becoming Secretary of the Trinitarian Bible Society. He was a man of intense spirituality and made a number of outstanding contributions to biblical scholarship and broad-based evangelical Christianity.

Bullinger's Last Book

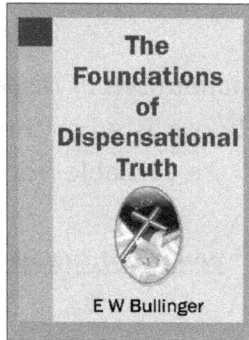

The
Foundations
of
Dispensational
Truth

E W Bullinger

The Foundations of Dispensation Truth

Bullinger's last book,
reflecting his mature views.

This is Bullinger's last book and is his definitive work on the subject of dispensationalism. It covers the ministries of ...

- the prophets,
- the Son of God,
- those that heard Christ, and
- the ministry of Paul, the Apostle to the Gentiles.

He comments on the Gospels and the Pauline epistles and has a lengthy section on the Acts of the Apostles, followed by one explaining why miraculous signs of the Acts period ceased.

This is a newly typeset book, well presented in an easy to read format.

Copies of *The Foundations of Dispensational Truth,*
and of the books listed on the next pages,
are available from

www.obt.org.uk

and from

The Open Bible Trust,
Fordland Mount, Upper Basildon,
Reading, RG8 8LU, UK.

They also available as eBooks
from Amazon Kindle and Apple,
and as KDP paperbacks from Amazon.

Also by Bullinger

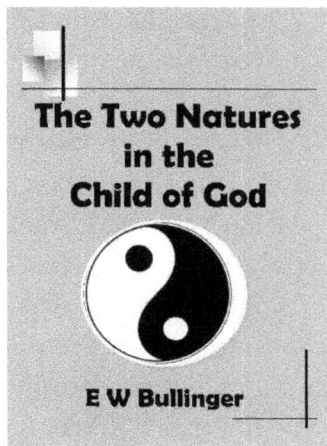

The Two Natures in the Child of God

The Bible sees the Christian as having an 'old nature', inherited through generation from Adam, and a 'new nature', bestowed through regeneration by God.

The names and characteristics of each are many and various, including "the natural man" and "the old man" over against "the divine nature" and "the new man".

The conflict between the two natures is discussed with details of our responsibilities regarding each, and the ultimate end of the old and new natures. Finally, practical suggestions are made for dealing with the old nature.

**Available as an eBook from Amazon and Apple
and as a KDP paperback from Amazon.**

The following is a selection of works by E W Bullinger published by The Open Bible Trust

The Transfiguration
The Knowledge of God
God's Purpose in Israel
The Prayers of Ephesians
The Lord's Day (Revelation 1:10)
The Rich Man and Lazarus
The Importance of Accuracy
Christ's Prophetic Teaching
The Resurrection of the Body
The Divine Names and Titles
The Spirits in Prison: 1 Peter 3:17-4:6
The Lesson of the Book of Job: The Oldest Lesson in the World
The Seven Sayings to the Woman at the Well
The Foundations of Dispensational Truth
The Christian's Greatest Need
Introducing the Church Epistles
The Two Natures in the Child of God
The Name of Jehovah in the Book of Esther
The Names and Order of the Books of the Old Testament
The Second Advent in Relation to the Jew
The Vision of Isaiah: Its Structure and Scope
The Importance of Accuracy: in the study of the Bible

More information about the above can be seen on www.obt.org.uk from where they can be ordered.

Further reading

Search magazine

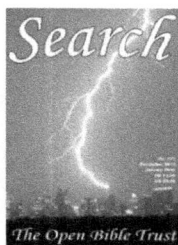

For a free sample of
the Open Bible Trust's magazine Search,
please email

admin@obt.org.uk

or visit

www.obt.org.uk/search

About this Book

The Potter's House
Interpretation & Applications

We must always seek the interpretation of a passage first, before we look for any applications. This is just what Bullinger does in this book.

He first of all gives us the interpterion of *The Potters* House, as found in Jeremiah 18:1-4, with respect to Israel. But then he seeks to apply it to Christians and the Church, and he has eight such applications.

1. The Covenants
2. Ordinances
3. The Priesthood
4. The Kings
5. Man
6. The Human Body
7. The Heavens and the Earth
8. The Church

His is a book which will make us look again at what goes on in Christendom today.

Publications of The Open Bible Trust must be in accordance with its evangelical, fundamental and dispensational basis. However, beyond this minimum, writers are free to express whatever beliefs they may have as their own understanding, provided that the aim in so doing is to further the object of The Open Bible Trust. A copy of the doctrinal basis is available on **www.obt.org.uk** or from:

THE OPEN BIBLE TRUST
Fordland Mount, Upper Basildon,
Reading, RG8 8LU, UK

www.ingramcontent.com/pod-product-compliance
Lightning Source LLC
Chambersburg PA
CBHW060722030426
42337CB00017B/2966